I Am Here

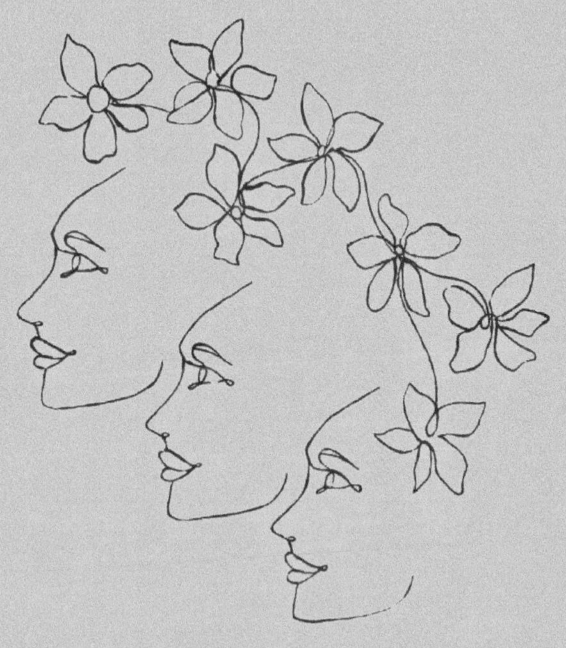

Thoughts From the Soul

Faith Aisien-Ezugwu

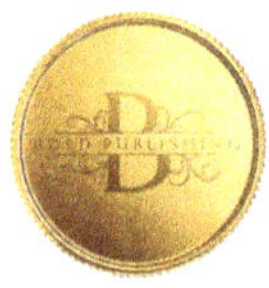

Table of Contents

"Often people attempt to live their lives backward; they try to have more things, or more money, in order to do more of what they want, so they will be happier. The way it actually works is the reverse. You must first be who you really are, then, do what you need to do, in order to have what you want."

~ Margaret Young

Dedication

Kelechi and Daluchi, my breath, my why, you are the oxygen in my lungs. You are my reason for being.

Onyemaechi, thank you for your unconditional love and support and for freeing me to express myself authentically.

Joseph, my father, I remember each life lesson you taught me and thank you posthumously. I have learned that to get anything of value one has to sacrifice.

For Emmanuella, my mother, your love and countless sacrifices will always be a beacon to my soul.

And to myself, I took a step forward. On this journey, I have found and secured my reason.

Acknowledgements

The author wishes to express gratitude to God for the gift of good health and for being a constant presence at every cornerstone of her life.

Alexandra Ohu thank you for putting my needs before yours. I appreciate you.

Thank you to my sisters for their sustained support - Eze Aisien, Mercy Edemeroh , Alexandra Ohu, Isoken Chumezie-Ideboh, Okunwa Okpala and Idia Aisien.

Aunty Deon thank you for being there and for championing my cause.

A special shout out to Ene Obi and the Ziano Mindspa community.

Alison Edwards, thanks for introducing me to the Common Grounds Poetic Club.

Kerry Scott of Kerry Scott Studios – I am immensely thankful for your invaluable assistance and support in bringing my imagination to life through the creation of the book cover.

Thank you for choosing this book. I penned these words straight from my heart. My sincere wish is that you enjoy reading it, finding inspiration, water to your souls and receive something meaningful.

Introduction

Within these pages, I explore self-reflection, self-discovery and the connections we share with others and the world around us.

This book encourages honesty and open dialogue about our thoughts, exposing the futility of judging ourselves through the lens of others.

Discover the stories of everyday life experiences that often go unspoken.

I welcome you to a corner of my world where you can explore and connect with the realities we often reserve for ourselves.

Immerse yourself in these pages as we navigate the journey of personal realisation; sharing in the unspoken moments that shape our lives.

Thank you for choosing *I Am Here*.

Searching

I Am Here

I am here, but you can't see me.

I am here, but you can't hear me.

What can I do to be heard?

I am desperate. Longing to fit in.

My hands are raised, but you can't see me.

When I strive to speak, you silence me.

What can I do to make you hear me?

What can I do to make you see me?

I want to share my heart with you,
but I am unseen.

I long to share my ideas with you,
but I am unheard.

I am here to explore.

I am here.

I am unseen.

I See You

I see you.

I see your pain, stress and struggles.

I see your effort.

I see your laughter.

I see your tears.

You are not alone.

I SEE YOU.

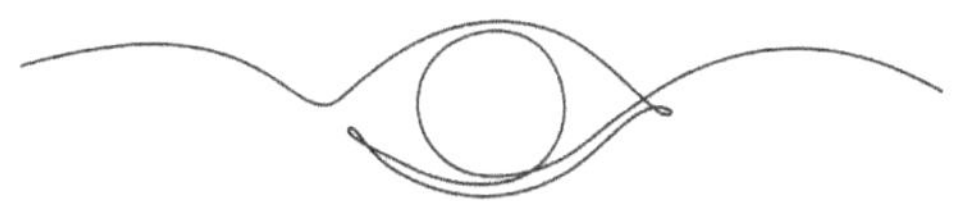

Dis-Ability

A lifetime of carrying a burden from birth.

There is no shame in having a dis-ability.

We are often made to feel excluded and out of place.

Why *are* we made to feel excluded and out of place?

Our dis-ability is what makes us who we are and what we are.

We work twice as hard behind closed doors to camouflage the cracks.

We always show up and give more.

Let's remove the shackles.

We *do* belong.

Find your space and flourish with your imperfection.

It's not a dis-ability.

It's a different ability.

Love - Part 1

Love is intimacy.

Love is passion.

Love is intoxicating.

Love is power.

Love is liberating.

Love is speechless commitment.

Love - Part 2

What is love?

Love is all around you.

Love is here.

Love is there.

Love is all around you.

If you choose to look closer,

It's right there.

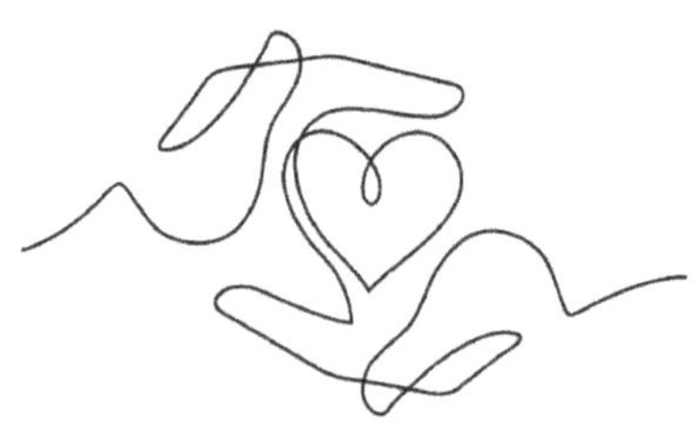

Broken

A Silent Loss

The hopes and joys we carry inside us,

We can't wait to share for another three months.

My excitement grows day-by-day of what it is I will birth.

Each day I wake with the thrill of the life inside me.

We meet family and friends. Not yet sharing the news.

I wake in the middle of the night.

I am soaked in a pool of blood.

OH. NO. I gasp, silently,

Accepting that this is the end.

I wait for news in a side room.

I am told this happens a lot.

Both hands are held and comforted.

We share no words for some time.

Our excitement dissipates.

Soundless, for days and days.

We never spoke of our silent LOSS.

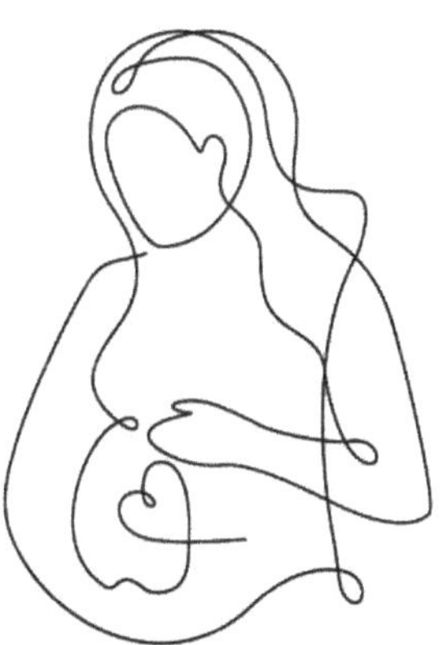

Raw

R - **R**age.

    A - **A**shamed.

        W - **W**orthy.

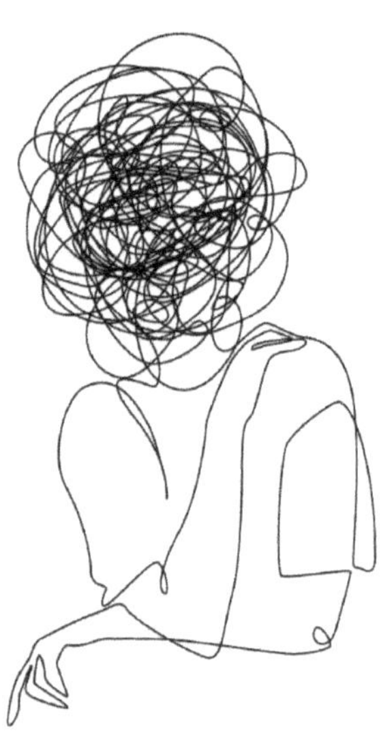

Faith Aisien-Ezugwu

You Don't Have to
Hurt Me to Win

You don't have to hurt me to win.

Your words hurt like a needle piercing through
a cloth with no end.

You pulled the plug, minus warning, because it
suits *you*.

There is no blame here and no turning back.

Those words remain. Eternal.

Even when we heal, the
scars are still present.

Our words live on, even
when we are gone.

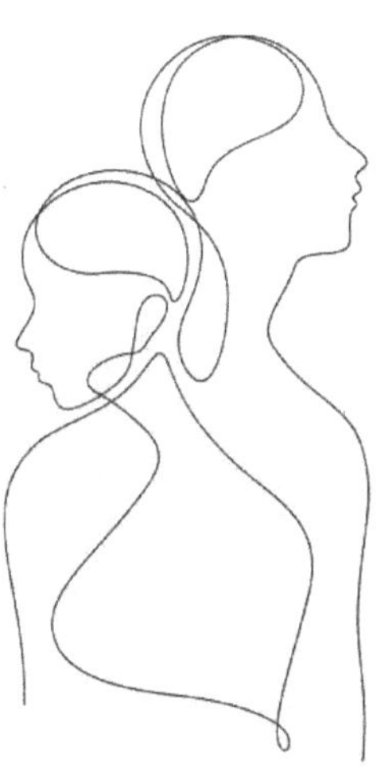

There are no winners here.

We both lost.

Acceptance

Acceptance is embracing what is, not what was, or what could have been.

Acceptance is listening to your voice.

Acceptance is knowing who you are.

Acceptance is loving who you are.

Acceptance is living in the present.

Acceptance is living and inhaling without regrets.

Acceptance is moving towards.

Finding

Boundaries

Boundaries are set from a place of love, not hate.

My words were not twisted and bitter.

They were simply words.

Boundaries are not meant to cause a divide,

But to enhance and enrich a relationship.

Don't judge me for my honesty. It came from a place of love.

I still stand by my words.

Boundaries come from a place of **love**.

Freedom

Freedom is expression without limitations.

Freedom is contentment.

Freedom is acceptance.

Freedom is laughter.

Freedom is weeping.

Freedom is strength.

Freedom is love.

What does freedom mean to YOU?

I Did It My Way

Through the highs and lows, the laughter and tears,

I trod the path less travelled, conquering my fears.

"I did it my way," a mantra embraced.

A journey unique, in my own grace.

With every sunrise, a canvas anew,

I painted my story in shades of true pink.

The winds of change, they whispered and roared.

I stumbled.

I fell.

Still I found the grace.

To rise again.

Discovered in life's endless maze.

In the face of doubts, no footsteps to follow,

I found my voice, carving my destiny;

A journey well designed.

I did it my way.

Through joy and sorrow,

Come what may,

I can say with conviction,

"I did it my way."

A Seat at My Table

You are *always* welcome here.

In a state of warmth and cheer

A table stands - so near and dear.

Its sturdy legs, like family strong,

Embrace us all where we belong.

Gather round, both young and old,

With stories to be shared and told.

Laughter echoes, gentle and kind,

Creating memories intertwined.

What is life if not for these,

These moments shared and hearts at ease?

A feast of love in every morsel,

Nurturing bonds, so sweet and immortal.

Through highs and lows, we navigate,

Uplifting one another, day by day.

No matter what the journey presents, rough or stable,

You will always have a seat at my table.

I Wish You Well

I wish you well as each day feasts
on the sun.

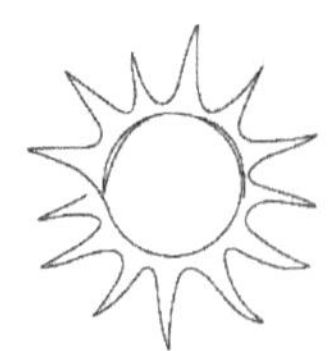

I wish you well, as a bee needs
bee balm.

I wish you well, as a plant that thirsts for
water.

I wish you well, as a vein needs blood.

I wish you well from every angle of life.

I wish you well today and always.

I wish you well.

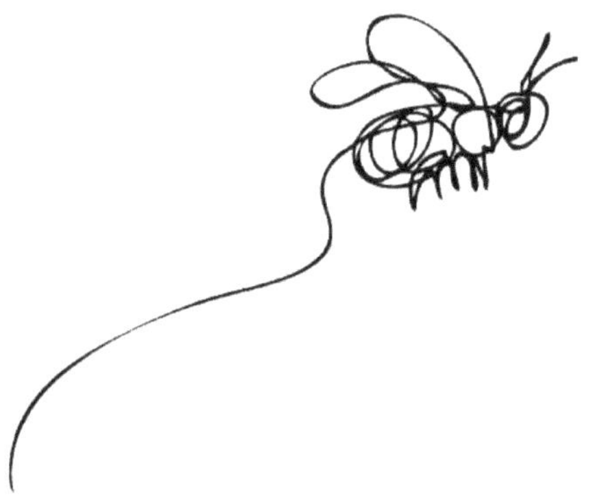

Connecting

Glasses

In frames, I view this world.

Behind the glass, I am unobserved.

A barrier between total light and me,

Leaves me feeling hidden from sight.

Eyes exposed to critical gaze.

I long to cast these spectacles away.

But then I see the world so clear,

I realise there's nothing to fear.

I embrace the lenses perched upon my nose,

For they show the world in truth.

With clarity and insight, I now see.

The beauty that comes from being me.

Faith Aisien-Ezugwu

Mirror Reflection

You are amazing, beautiful, consistent,

diligent, empowered, fulfilled,

gracious, hopeful, intelligent,

joyful, kind, loyal,

magnificent, noble, omnipotent,

peaceful, quintessential, reliable,

sincere, thoughtful, useful,

versatile, worthy, xenial,

youthful,

zealous.

That *is* you looking back at me.

A Year of Flowers To Me

January blooms in the winter's chill,

snowdrops whisper, a silent thrill.

February brings the crocus bright.

March dances with daffodils fair.

April showers, tulips arise.

May unfolds with the lily's beauty.

June sees roses in full bloom.

July brings daisies, pure and white.

August warms with sunflowers tall.

September whispers dahlias' tale.

October chrysanthemums take the stage.

November asters, a hushed bloom.

December, holly in festive attire,

a year of flowers brings joy to the soul.

Faith Aisien-Ezugwu

A Happy Place

Amidst the chaos of the world external,

Lies a haven where my heart resides.

A place of peace, most secure.

A refuge where my spirit endures.

In my happy habitat, nature's beauty thrives,

Under the open sky, where the soul revives.

The gentle rustle of leaves in the breeze,

Brings a sense of calm, puts my heart at ease.

Beneath the shade of a towering tree,

Its branches, like arms, embrace my core.

In this sanctuary, I am complete.

In my happy place, time seems slow

Just as a river's current flows,

Bringing tranquillity to this sacred space.

The sun casts its warm and golden light,

Wrapping me in it's comforting might.

In this haven, my inner joy ignites.

Here, I find solace in the rustling leaves,

As my heart in this moment perceives.

In my happy place, I know I will shine.

In this land of nature and grace,

I'm surrounded, embraced, in this sacred place.

My happy place is where my spirit is free.

Faith Aisien-Ezugwu

My Mother - Iya Mi

A pillar of strength with gentle hands.

Her love, an endless tide

Flowing through my life as a constant guide.

My mother. A portrait of sacrifice and grace.

Enduring each trial with a steadfast embrace.

Shining through darkness as a guiding light.

Through thundery days and nights so long,

She stands unwavering, steadfast and strong.

Putting herself last, her love is profound.

My mother. An embodiment of grace.

A determined presence in this life's race.

Guiding me through every dream.

In her eyes, I see love for her children.

A love that will forever endure.

She sacrifices a gift beyond measure.

So here I stand, in awe of

Love so pure, a mother's grace.

In the heart of my memories, she stands.

My mother. Iya Mi.

Faith Aisien-Ezugwu

Sisters

There's a bond so rare.

My sisters are beyond compare,

Support like no other.

In the depths of their eyes is an unspoken word,

A commitment strong, through thick and thin.

Through laughter and tears, as days unfold,

Their togetherness, a comforting embrace,

Sharing secrets, worries and dreams unvoiced.

Through the peaks and valleys, they stand side
by side,

In times of bliss, they celebrate with joy,

In moments of sorrow, they find a way,

Sisters forever, an unbreakable chain.

So here's to the sisters, a gift from above,

A bond so profound, an unspoken love.

Through storms and sunshine, they'll always be.

An anchor.

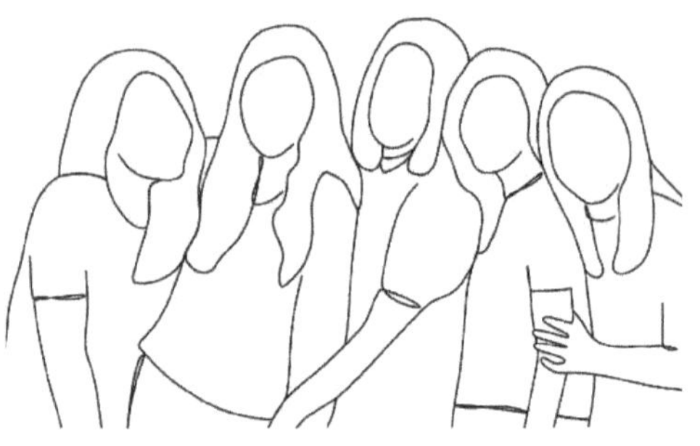

Now

September

Ninth month of the calendar year.

Harvest time, fields align.

New beginnings.

A season's start.

Dahlias blooms like works of art.

Sapphire stones, a symbol of wisdom and loyalty.

September love.

May it find you as it found me.

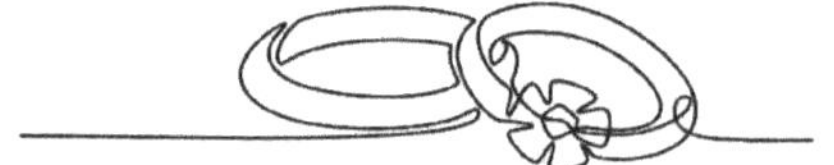

Breath

Breathe.

Breathe.

BREATHE.

Be Still

Take a moment to be still.

To release.

To dream.

To feel.

To love.

To be.

Be still and know

I am **God**.

Faith Aisien-Ezugwu

I Am Here

I Am Here.

I Am Loved.

I Am Seen.

And

I Belong

To **me**.

The Dot

●

*-You can write yourself a new ending
starting from today-*

-Notes-

*Use these following pages for whatever you wish;
write, explore, create, reflect...*

-Notes-

-Notes-

-Notes-

About the Author

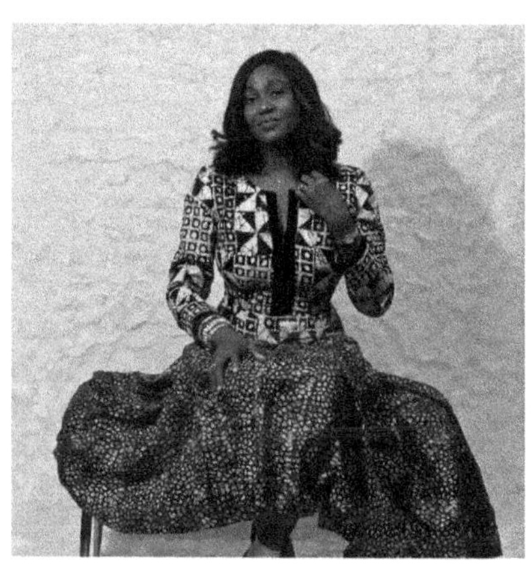

Faith Aisien-Ezugwu is a graduate of Greenwich University and the University of Hull. Her undergraduate and postgraduate studies in Business and Events Management set the stage for her professional journey.

With over 20 years of experience, Faith began her career as an executive in customer service management and later transitioned to project management and patient experience within the health sector.

Faith is an advocate for charitable causes. She is dedicated to supporting sickle cell anemia, raising funds through annual events.

Beyond her professional life, Faith finds joy in the world of art and music, appreciating diverse genres.

She resides in Kent, United Kingdom, sharing her life with her husband and two children, cherishing each moment with her loved ones.